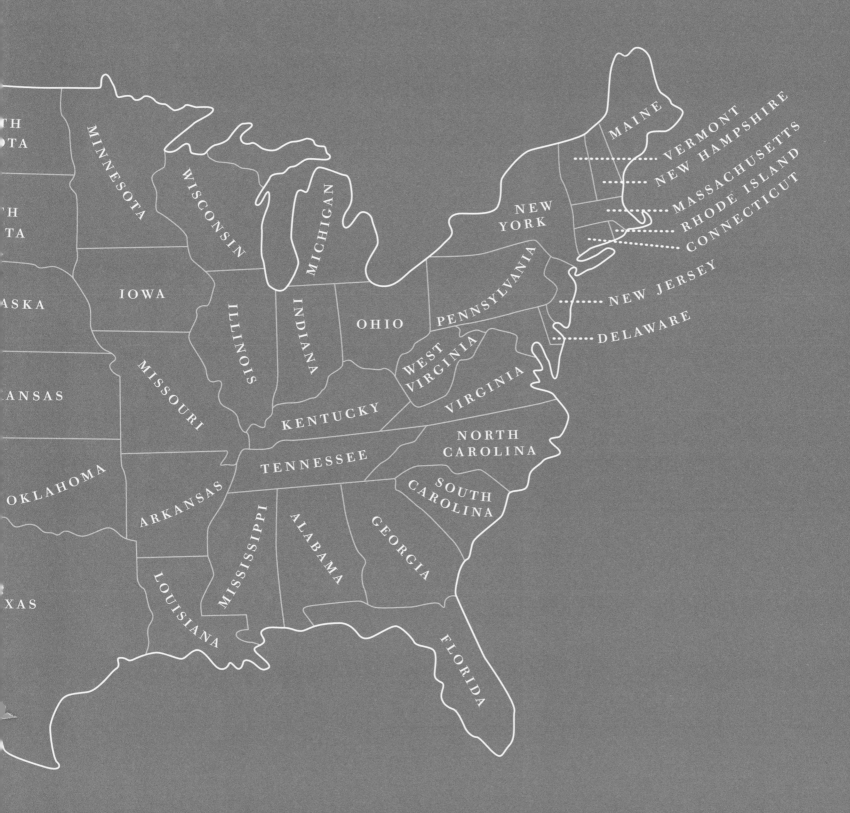

Thermador® | *An American Icon*™

TASTE OF AMERICA

The Great American Oven Cookbook

CELEBRATING

50 YEARS

OF THE
BUILT-IN OVEN
CREATED BY
Thermador®

50 States • 50 Recipes

ISBN 1-4243-0104-1

Printed in Korea

Conception, Art Direction & Production: Hamon & Associates

Thermador Brand Manager: Beatriz Sandoval

Editor: Karen Kaplan

Photographer: Brian Leatart

Food Stylist: Maggie Ward

Recipe Tester: Jeanne Kelley

Copy Editor: Amy Steinberg

Indexer: Tricia Callas O'Donnell

On the cover: Peach Cobbler (page 26)

Thermador® | *An American Icon*™

TASTE OF AMERICA

The Great American Oven Cookbook

Recipe Selection by Chef Bradley Ogden

Karen Kaplan, *Editor*

Brian Leatart, *Photographer*

Maggie Ward, *Food Stylist*

50 States • 50 Recipes

A COOKBOOK 50 YEARS IN THE MAKING

The 50th Anniversary of the Built-In Oven In 1955, 20 years after becoming one of the preeminent manufacturers of kitchen appliances in the country, Thermador invented the first built-in wall oven and forever changed the concept of the American kitchen. This revolutionary design's convenience and flexibility were quickly embraced by home chefs throughout the country, permanently establishing Thermador's reputation as the preferred brand for the cooking enthusiast. That development five decades ago, like everything we do here at Thermador, was driven by our passion for cooking excellence, and our ongoing quest to empower our customers to create the finest meals for their family and friends. It's in this spirit that we present a collection of 50 delicious recipes from across America, hand-picked for their culinary merit.

50 Years, 50 States, 50 Recipes We invited home chefs from around the country to help celebrate the anniversary of our invention of the built-in oven by submitting their favorite recipes to our "Taste of America" contest. Every recipe submitted was judged by a panel of experts, led by world-renowned chef Bradley Ogden, on taste, originality, and how well it represented its region. The best recipes were chosen, one representing each state, for inclusion in this book. You owe it to yourself to give each of these wonderful recipes a try. Like Thermador, they truly represent the best that America has to offer.

CHEF OGDEN

I want to thank Thermador for giving me this opportunity to select 50 American oven recipes to be included in this cookbook. It never ceases to amaze me how wonderfully diverse and original our nation's cuisine is, and I believe this book is a delightful celebration of its endless variety, as well as a tribute to the culinary enthusiasts from around the country who submitted these recipes.

Bradley Ogden is a James Beard Foundation-recognized chef and a graduate of the Culinary Institute of America. He first rose to prominence with his "farm-fresh" American cuisine at the renowned Campton Place Hotel in San Francisco before opening his signature restaurant, The Lark Creek Inn in Marin County. This was followed by One Market in San Francisco, Lark Creek in Walnut Creek, Yankee Pier in Larkspur, Parcel 104 in Santa Clara, and Arterra in Del Mar. He was named Chef of the Year by the Culinary Institute of America, as well as one of the Great American Chefs by the International Wine and Food Society. His latest venture is his eponymous restaurant at Caesars Palace, Las Vegas, which was named Best New Restaurant 2004 by the James Beard Foundation.

Crepe Lasagna, page 66

CONTENTS

GULF COAST SHRIMP
WITH SWEET TOMATO RELISH

Shrimp from the Gulf Coast are famous for their delectability. According to Helen, shrimp seem more typical of Alabama than cotton bales or magnolias in the moonlight. Here, they're paired with a tomato relish sweetened with local cane syrup or molasses in a dish inspired by Shrimp de Jonghe, a specialty she ate in Chicago during the forties.

6 to 8 servings

Relish
1½ cups diced fresh tomatoes
¼ cup thinly sliced green onions (white part only)
2 tablespoons minced fresh cilantro
1 tablespoon cane syrup or light molasses
1 tablespoon fresh lemon juice
Salt

Shrimp
½ cup (1 stick) butter, divided
2 cups fresh breadcrumbs made from white bread
½ teaspoon chili powder
Salt

½ cup dry Sherry
2 tablespoons fresh lemon juice
½ cup sliced green onions (green part only)
¼ cup minced fresh parsley
4 garlic cloves, pressed
1 teaspoon salt
½ teaspoon chili powder
2 pounds uncooked large shrimp, peeled, deveined
Additional sliced green onions (green part only; optional)

Submitted by:
HELEN CONWELL

For relish: Combine first 5 ingredients in nonmetal bowl. Season with salt. Let stand at room temperature until ready to use.

For shrimp: Preheat oven to 350°F. Melt ¼ cup (½ stick) butter in heavy medium skillet over medium heat. Add breadcrumbs and sauté until beginning to turn golden brown, about 2 minutes. Add chili powder. Season to taste with salt.

Melt remaining ¼ cup (½ stick) butter in heavy large skillet over medium heat. Remove from heat. Stir in

Sherry and next 6 ingredients. Add shrimp and turn to coat. Transfer shrimp mixture to shallow 2-quart casserole dish or 13x9-inch baking dish, arranging shrimp in single layer, overlapping slightly if necessary. Spread breadcrumb mixture over shrimp. Bake until shrimp are pink and crumbs are golden, about 30 minutes. Garnish with additional sliced green onions if desired. Serve immediately with relish.

Serve with white wine, such as Sauvignon Blanc.

CREAMY HALIBUT DIP
WITH SERRANO CHILE

Alaskan halibut is world-renowned and prized by connoisseurs everywhere, so it's not surprising that John, a onetime chef, would take advantage of its sweet flesh in this clever spread. Serve it with bread, crackers, tortilla chips, or with raw or blanched vegetables.

2 tablespoons olive oil
1 sweet onion (such as Maui or Vidalia), minced
2 garlic cloves, minced
Salt and freshly ground black pepper
1 8-ounce halibut fillet, cut into
   ½-inch-thick slices
½ cup mayonnaise
¼ cup fresh breadcrumbs made from white bread

½ cup sour cream
1 serrano chile, minced
1 tablespoon minced fresh cilantro
Fresh cilantro sprigs

Makes about 2½ cups

Preheat oven to 400°F. Heat oil in heavy medium ovenproof skillet over medium-high heat. Add onion and garlic and sauté until tender and golden, about 8 minutes. Season with salt and pepper. Arrange halibut slices in single layer atop onion mixture. Season with salt and pepper. Spread mayonnaise atop halibut, then sprinkle with breadcrumbs. Bake until fish is cooked through, about 10 minutes. Transfer mixture to serving bowl. Cool, then refrigerate until chilled.

Using fork, stir sour cream, serrano chile, and minced cilantro into halibut mixture, making sure to break up fish. Season with salt and pepper. Garnish with cilantro sprigs. (Can be prepared 1 day ahead. Cover and refrigerate.)

Serve with white wine, such as Chardonnay.

Submitted by:
JOHN ST. MARTIN

TOASTED MEATLOAF MELT
WITH AVOCADO SALSA & CILANTRO MAYONNAISE

Jenny, a card-carrying foodie, was inspired by the explosive flavors of the Southwest and by her grandmother's meatloaf to create this refined yet still rustic sandwich.

6 servings

Meatloaf
- 1 pound lean ground beef
- ½ cup garlic-and-herb dry breadcrumbs
- ¼ cup finely chopped onion
- ¼ cup finely chopped green bell pepper
- 1 large egg, beaten to blend
- 1 4-ounce can diced green chilies
- 1 teaspoon Tabasco sauce
- ½ teaspoon salt
- ¼ teaspoon freshly ground black pepper
- 1 garlic clove, pressed

Mayonnaise
- ½ cup mayonnaise
- ¼ cup chopped fresh cilantro leaves
- 1 teaspoon ground cumin
- Freshly ground black pepper

Salsa
- 2 ripe avocados, peeled, seeded, diced into ½-inch cubes
- ⅔ cup diced firm tomato
- ½ cup finely diced red onion
- ¼ cup chopped fresh cilantro leaves
- 2 tablespoons fresh lime juice
- ½ teaspoon ground cumin
- 1 garlic clove, pressed
- Salt and freshly ground black pepper

Assembly
- 6 8x4½-inch slices sourdough bread, toasted, halved
- 6 slices cheddar cheese

Submitted by:
JENNY FLAKE

For meatloaf: Preheat oven to 350°F. Oil 8x5-inch loaf pan. Combine all ingredients in large bowl; gently mix until just blended. Shape into 7x4½-inch loaf and place in prepared pan. Bake until meatloaf is cooked through and top is browned, about 40 minutes. Cool 10 minutes. Cut into ½-inch slices. (Can be prepared 1 day ahead. Cool completely, wrap, and refrigerate. To reheat, arrange slices on baking sheet and broil until heated through.)

For mayonnaise: Mix first 3 ingredients in bowl. Season with pepper. Cover and refrigerate. (Can be prepared up to 3 days ahead.)

For salsa: Combine first 7 ingredients in bowl. Season with salt and pepper. Toss salsa gently. Cover and refrigerate. (Can be prepared up to 8 hours ahead.)

To assemble: Preheat broiler. Set all bread slices on baking sheet. Cover half of bread slices with cheese slices. Broil until cheese melts. Top cheese with meatloaf. Cover meatloaf with salsa. Spread mayonnaise on remaining bread slices. Top meatloaf with bread, mayonnaise side down. Serve immediately.

Serve with beer.

CINNAMON ROLLS
WITH CREAM CHEESE FROSTING

The baking tradition is an important one in the state of Arkansas. This recipe is a perfect example: It belonged to Trish's grandmother, who gave it to Trish's mom, who gave it to Trish. These rolls are wonderful for breakfast, for brunch, or as an anytime treat.

Makes 12

Dough
½ cup (1 stick) butter
1 cup whole milk
¼ cup sugar
1 teaspoon salt

2 ¼-ounce packages dry yeast
⅓ cup warm water

3 large eggs, beaten to blend
1 cup instant mashed potato flakes
4 cups all purpose flour

Filling
1 cup (firmly packed) golden brown sugar
2 teaspoons ground cinnamon
½ cup (1 stick) butter

Frosting
1 cup powdered sugar
2 ounces cream cheese, chilled
1 tablespoon whole milk
½ teaspoon vanilla extract

For dough: Melt butter in heavy small skillet over medium-high heat. Add milk, sugar, and salt and bring just to simmer. Pour into bowl of heavy-duty mixer fitted with dough hook. Cool to lukewarm.

Meanwhile, sprinkle yeast over ⅓ cup warm water in small bowl. Stir to dissolve.

Beat yeast mixture and eggs into milk mixture. Mix in potato flakes. Beat in flour 1 cup at a time. Transfer dough to floured work surface and knead until smooth. Transfer dough to oiled bowl; turn to coat. Cover with damp cloth and let rise in warm draft-free area until doubled in volume, about 1½ hours.

For filling: Mix brown sugar and cinnamon in bowl. Melt butter in heavy small saucepan. Roll dough out on lightly floured surface to 14x9-inch rectangle

about 1 inch thick. Brush dough generously with melted butter. Sprinkle evenly with brown sugar mixture. Beginning at 1 long end, roll up dough jelly-roll style. Cut into 12 equal pieces. Arrange on baking sheets. Let rise in warm draft-free area until doubled in volume, about 20 minutes.

Preheat oven to 350°F. Brush roll tops with remaining melted butter. Bake until cooked through and slightly golden, about 12 minutes. Transfer to rack and cool completely.

For frosting: Using electric mixer, beat all ingredients until smooth. Drizzle rolls with frosting just before serving.

Serve with coffee, tea, milk, hot chocolate, or juice.

Submitted by:
TRISH WALLER

GOLDEN VALLEY OVEN CHICKEN

Oranges, wine, garlic, almonds, and sourdough bread—just some of California's luscious bounty—inspired Michelle to create this sophisticated chicken breast dish. Serve with a lightly dressed salad of baby greens.

4 servings

1 navel orange
½ cup dry white wine
6 7-ounce skinless boneless chicken breasts, pounded to ½-inch thickness

2 cups fresh breadcrumbs made from sourdough bread
½ cup almonds, chopped
2 garlic cloves, pressed
6 tablespoons (¾ stick) butter, melted, divided
Salt and freshly ground black pepper

2 teaspoons cornstarch
Pinch of sugar

Submitted by:
MICHELLE SEYMOUR

Grate ½ teaspoon peel from orange (reserve remaining peel for another use if desired). Juice orange (yield should be about ½ cup juice). Combine ½ teaspoon peel, ½ cup juice, and white wine in large glass baking dish. Add chicken; turn to coat with marinade. Let stand at least 30 minutes or cover and refrigerate overnight.

Preheat oven to 350°F. Combine breadcrumbs, almonds, and garlic in another baking dish. Stir in 4 tablespoons melted butter. Season with salt and pepper. Bake until mixture is golden brown, stirring occasionally, about 10 minutes. Transfer breadcrumb

mixture to plate. Wipe baking dish clean. Remove chicken from marinade; reserve marinade. Brush each chicken breast with some of remaining melted butter. Season with salt and pepper. Coat each breast completely in breadcrumb mixture. Arrange chicken in clean baking dish. Bake 35 minutes.

Transfer reserved marinade to heavy small saucepan. Stir in cornstarch and pinch of sugar. Season with salt and pepper. Bring to boil, then simmer until thickened. Serve with chicken.

Serve with white wine, such as Chardonnay.

WESTERN SLOPE PEAR & GINGER CAKE

The O'Connor clan, who run a large catering firm in Denver, love this cake, which takes advantage of scrumptious pears from Colorado's Grand Junction area. The recipe was passed down from Pat's grandmother; Pat added pear liqueur to spice things up a bit. Serve it warm with vanilla ice cream or whipped cream.

8 servings

Cake
Butter for pie dish
- 1 cup all purpose flour
- 1 teaspoon ground ginger
- ¼ teaspoon salt
- 6 tablespoons (¾ stick) butter, room temperature
- ⅔ cup (firmly packed) golden brown sugar
- 1 tablespoon grated peeled fresh ginger
- 2 large eggs
- ¾ cup whole milk
- 3 tablespoons pear liqueur

Topping
- 2 firm but ripe pears
- 1 tablespoon melted butter
- 2 tablespoons (firmly packed) golden brown sugar
- ¼ teaspoon ground ginger
Powdered sugar

For cake: Preheat oven to 350°F. Butter 9-inch-diameter pie dish. Combine flour, ground ginger, and salt in small bowl. Using electric mixer, cream butter, brown sugar, and fresh ginger in medium bowl. Add eggs 1 at a time, beating well after each addition. Beat in milk and pear liqueur. Beat in flour mixture. Spread batter in prepared dish.

For topping: Peel and core pears. Cut into quarters, then cut quarters into slices. Arrange pear slices in spoke pattern on batter. Brush pears with melted butter. Mix brown sugar and ginger in small bowl. Sprinkle over pears. Bake cake until browned and tester inserted near center comes out clean, about 50 minutes. Sprinkle immediately with powdered sugar. Serve warm.

Submitted by:
PAT O'CONNOR

Serve with coffee, tea, pear eau-de-vie, or pear cider.

YANKEE POT ROAST

Connecticut is called the Nutmeg State because in olden times unscrupulous peddlers used to try to sell wooden versions of the spice to unwary housewives. This soul-satisfying recipe calls for the real thing, freshly grated if possible. Steven says the aroma of this dish makes his house smell like his childhood Connecticut home.

8 servings

1 teaspoon dried thyme
1 teaspoon freshly grated nutmeg
1 teaspoon celery salt
1 teaspoon coarse salt
½ teaspoon freshly ground black pepper
4 pounds beef rump roast, room temperature
1 large onion, thickly sliced
1 cup beef broth
2 tablespoons apple cider vinegar
1 bay leaf

2 pounds (about 4) large carrots, peeled, halved lengthwise

Fresh celery leaves (for garnish)

Submitted by:
STEVEN CARTHY

Preheat oven to 350°F. Mix first 5 ingredients in small bowl. Rub spice mixture all over beef. Line bottom of large Dutch oven with onion slices. Place beef, fat side up, atop onions. Bring broth to boil in heavy small saucepan. Pour broth over beef. Add vinegar and bay leaf. Cover and roast 1 hour.

Reduce oven temperature to 300°F. Add carrots to Dutch oven, cover, and roast until beef and carrots are fork-tender, about 2 hours.

Cool beef in pan at least 10 minutes. Transfer beef to cutting board and slice against grain. (Can be prepared 1 day ahead. Cover and refrigerate. Defat and reheat before serving.) Place on platter. Garnish with carrots and celery leaves.

Serve with red wine, such as Zinfandel.

21

SPICY GRATIN OF CRAB

Luscious Delaware crab is featured in this sinfully rich shellfish main course that was devised by Cheri especially for the Thermador contest. Cooking is Cheri's hobby, and she started entering cooking competitions a few years ago.

Butter for gratin dishes
¼ cup (½ stick) butter
1½ cups chopped Vidalia onion
1⅓ cups chopped celery
1 cup chopped green bell pepper
4 garlic cloves, minced

¼ cup all purpose flour
2 cups whole milk
2 teaspoons Cajun/Creole seasoning
1 pound fresh crabmeat, picked over
½ cup heavy cream
¾ cup freshly grated Parmesan cheese

6 servings

Preheat oven to 400°F. Butter six 1-cup gratin dishes. Melt ¼ cup butter in heavy large saucepan over medium-high heat. Add onion, celery, bell pepper, and garlic and sauté until tender, about 5 minutes. Reduce heat to medium-low. Add flour and stir 3 minutes. Slowly stir in milk. Cook until thickened, stirring often, about 3 minutes. Add seasoning and stir 2 minutes.

Add crab and cream and stir to blend. Transfer mixture to prepared gratin dishes. (Can be prepared 4 hours ahead. Cover and refrigerate.) Sprinkle 2 tablespoons Parmesan cheese atop crab mixture in each dish. Bake 20 minutes. Serve immediately.

Serve with beer.

Submitted by:
CHERI AUTHEMENT

ROASTED GROUPER & YELLOW PEPPERS
WITH KEY LIME, HERBS & SPICES

Black grouper and Key limes are two of Florida's favorite ingredients, and they're shown off beautifully in this refined main course. The creator of this recipe, professional chef Fred Lucardie, likes to serve it with polenta and sautéed mushrooms, but it is also delicious on its own, or accompanied by white rice, roasted new potatoes, or crusty bread.

4 servings

Fish
- 2 tablespoons medium-dry Sherry (such as Dry Sack)
- 2 tablespoons extra-virgin olive oil
- 1 tablespoon fresh lime juice (preferably from Key limes)
- 1 tablespoon chopped fresh parsley
- 1 tablespoon chopped fresh cilantro
- 1 garlic clove, pressed
- 1 teaspoon freshly ground black pepper
- ½ teaspoon Hungarian sweet paprika
- ½ teaspoon fine sea salt
- ¼ teaspoon ground mace

Pinch of saffron threads
- 4 6-ounce black grouper or orange roughy fillets (each about 1¾ inches thick)

Peppers
- 2 yellow bell peppers

Olive oil

- 2 tablespoons extra-virgin olive oil
- 1 tablespoon fresh lime juice (preferably from Key limes)
- 1 tablespoon Sherry wine vinegar
- 1 tablespoon chopped fresh parsley
- 1 tablespoon chopped fresh cilantro
- ½ teaspoon Hungarian sweet paprika
- ¼ teaspoon ground mace

Pinch of saffron threads

- 4 lime wedges (preferably from Key limes)
- 4 fresh parsley sprigs
- 4 fresh cilantro sprigs

Submitted by:
FRED LUCARDIE

For fish: Combine first 11 ingredients in baking dish. Add fish; turn to coat. Cover and refrigerate at least 2 hours or overnight.

For peppers: Preheat oven to 350°F. Coat whole peppers with olive oil and place on baking sheet. Bake until peppers are tender, about 30 minutes. Maintain oven temperature. Transfer peppers to bowl. Cover with plastic wrap. Let stand until cool.

Peel, stem, and seed peppers. Cut into strips; place pepper strips in bowl. Add 2 tablespoons olive oil and next 7 ingredients and toss to coat. (Can be prepared up to 2 days ahead. Cover and refrigerate.)

Transfer fish from marinade to another baking dish. Bake until cooked through, about 20 minutes. Serve with peppers. Garnish with lime and herbs.

Serve with white wine, such as dry Riesling.

PEACH COBBLER

Nothing says Georgia like peaches, and nothing says peaches like cobbler. This easy-as-pie recipe was passed down to Wendie from her grandmother Genell Douglas. The family has been in the Peach State for many generations.

Butter for pan
2 pounds ripe peaches (about 5 medium)
1 cup whole milk
1 cup self-rising flour

¾ cup sugar
½ cup (1 stick) chilled unsalted butter, cut into small pieces

6 servings

Preheat oven to 350°F. Butter 9x5x2½-inch loaf pan. Peel and slice peaches (yield should be about 5 cups). Place peach slices in prepared pan. Whisk milk, flour, and sugar in medium bowl. Pour over peaches. Dot mixture with butter pieces. Bake until cobbler is browned in center, about 1½ hours. Serve immediately.

Serve with coffee or tea.

Submitted by:
WENDIE McCONNELL

ISLAND FIRE-AND-ICE PULLED PORK
WITH MANGO SALSA

Pineapple, Maui onions, shoyu, honey, and ginger are some of the explosive island flavors that come together in this outstanding main course invented by Kara, a foodie who rarely enters cooking competitions, but when she does, she wins. Accompany it with white rice, and garnish with fresh pineapple.

8 servings

Marinade
2 cups pineapple juice
¾ cup shoyu or soy sauce
¼ cup balsamic vinegar
2 tablespoons olive oil
2 tablespoons honey
4 teaspoons grated peeled fresh ginger
1 Maui onion, finely chopped
1 bunch cilantro, chopped (stems included)
3 fresh jalapeño chiles, seeded, chopped
8 garlic cloves, minced
1 4- to 5-pound pork butt

Mango Salsa
2 large fresh mangoes, cut into ¼-inch pieces
1 cup chopped Maui onion
¾ cup chopped fresh cilantro leaves
¾ cup fresh lime juice
1 teaspoon grated lime peel
1 teaspoon whole coriander seeds, lightly toasted, crushed slightly in mortar with pestle
2 garlic cloves, minced
Salt and freshly ground black pepper

Submitted by:
KARA ADANALIAN

For marinade: Combine first 10 ingredients in large pot or Dutch oven; stir to blend. Add pork. Cover and refrigerate overnight, turning pork once.

Preheat oven to 325°F. Pour off and reserve half of marinade from pork. Roast pork 3 ½ hours, adding reserved marinade as needed to keep pork moist.

Meanwhile, for salsa: Combine first 7 ingredients in bowl. Season salsa with salt and pepper. Cover and refrigerate up to 2 hours.

Cool meat slightly. Pull and shred meat, discarding any unrendered fat. Add any remaining reserved marinade to pot. Boil marinade until onions are tender, about 4 minutes. Return pork to pot. Roast uncovered until slightly crisp, 10 to 15 minutes. (Can be prepared 2 days ahead. Cover and refrigerate. Reheat in 325°F oven.) Serve with salsa.

Serve with red wine, such as Syrah.

SNAKE RIVER LAMB SHANKS

When the Basques came to Idaho they started a sheepherding tradition. Today the state is renowned for its tender lamb, and the meat is an integral part of the Idahoan kitchen. When Carter was growing up, lamb was on the table both at home and at his grandparents' restaurant. This recipe is a family one, which he has reworked over the years.

2 tablespoons olive oil

4 12-ounce lamb shanks

4 cups beef broth

3/4 cup sweet red vermouth

4 garlic cloves, chopped

1 tablespoon chopped fresh rosemary

Salt and freshly ground black pepper

1 medium white onion, chopped

12 ounces short pasta

3 tablespoons butter

4 servings

Preheat oven to 300°F. Heat olive oil in heavy large Dutch oven over medium heat. Add lamb shanks and brown well on both sides, about 7 minutes. Pour broth and vermouth over. Sprinkle with garlic and rosemary. Season with salt and pepper. Top with onion. Cover Dutch oven and roast until lamb is very tender, about 3 1/2 hours.

Transfer lamb from Dutch oven to ovenproof platter; cover lamb with foil. Return lamb to oven to keep warm. Set Dutch oven over high heat and bring pan juices to boil, scraping up browned bits with wooden spoon. Continue boiling until liquid is reduced to 1 3/4

cups, stirring occasionally, 5 to 10 minutes. (Can be prepared up to 3 days ahead. Cool. Cover and refrigerate in Dutch oven. Simmer over low heat to reheat.)

Meanwhile, bring large pot of salted water to boil. Cook pasta until tender but still firm to bite, stirring occasionally. Drain. Toss with butter. Divide pasta among 4 plates. Set 1 lamb shank atop pasta on each plate. Spoon pan juices over and serve.

Serve with red wine, such as Cabernet Sauvignon.

Submitted by:
CARTER WILSON

ILLINI BAKED BEANS
WITH BACON & SAUSAGE

Beans and bacon (not to mention sausage) are state staples, and here they're married in a rib-sticking dish. This American-style cassoulet keeps well, reheats beautifully, and is good warm or cool. Which makes it perfect for tailgating, a tradition that began, at least according to legend, at the University of Illinois, where Todd was the tailgate chairperson for his MBA class. Makes sense.

8 to 10 servings

1 pound bacon
1 pound mild Italian sausages
½ pound smoked hot sausage (such as andouille)
3 medium onions, chopped
½ cup (firmly packed) golden brown sugar
⅓ cup distilled white vinegar

2 tablespoons dry mustard
1 28-ounce can baked beans
1 15¼-ounce can lima beans
1 15-ounce can kidney beans
1 15-ounce can butter beans
1 14½-ounce can chicken broth

Submitted by:
TODD K. STANTON

Preheat oven to 325°F. Sauté bacon in Dutch oven over medium heat. Drain bacon on paper towels, then crumble bacon and set aside. Remove all but 3 tablespoons bacon drippings from Dutch oven. Add sausages to Dutch oven and brown well on all sides. Cool sausages slightly, then cut into rounds; set aside. Add onions to Dutch oven and sauté until just tender, about 10 minutes. Add brown sugar, vinegar, and mustard and simmer 2 minutes. Add bacon, sausage, all beans with their liquid, and chicken broth to Dutch oven. Cover and bake 2 hours. Serve immediately or at room temperature. (Can be prepared up to 3 days ahead. Cool, cover, and refrigerate. Stir gently over medium-low heat to reheat.)

Serve with beer.

CINNAMON-SUGAR
BREAKFAST PUFFS

Baking is a way of life in Indiana. The recipe for these ethereal morning treats was given to Darci by her mother, who got it from a cookbook. Darci added more butter to the batter and used nutmeg instead of cinnamon to make the puffs her own.

Butter for muffin cups
11 tablespoons butter, room temperature, divided
 1 cup sugar, divided
 1 large egg
1½ cups all purpose flour
1½ teaspoons baking powder
 ½ teaspoon salt
 ½ cup whole milk

1 teaspoon ground cinnamon

Makes 12

Preheat oven to 350°F. Butter 12 standard muffin cups. Using wooden spoon, beat 5 tablespoons butter, 1/2 cup sugar, and egg in large bowl. Combine flour, baking powder, and salt in another bowl. Stir flour mixture and milk alternately into butter-sugar mixture. Divide batter evenly among prepared muffin cups. Bake until puffs are golden brown, about 20 minutes.

Meanwhile, melt remaining 6 tablespoons butter in heavy small saucepan. Combine remaining 1/2 cup sugar and cinnamon on large plate. Roll hot puffs in melted butter, then in cinnamon sugar. Serve warm or at room temperature. (Can be prepared 1 day ahead. Store in airtight container.)

Serve with coffee, tea, milk, hot chocolate, or juice.

Submitted by:
DARCI MONTOVANI

UNCLE CHESTER'S
BLUE CHEESE TOASTS

America has a world-class blue-veined cheese in Newton, Iowa's Maytag blue. Uncle Chester may be long gone, but his legacy lives on in this old family recipe. Jim says that these bite-size appetizers are great for a cocktail party. The recipe doubles or triples easily if you're having a crowd.

Makes 16

4 slices whole grain or whole wheat bread
4 ounces Maytag blue cheese or other blue
   cheese, finely crumbled

¼ cup mayonnaise
2 tablespoons minced fresh chives
Pinch of cayenne pepper

Submitted by:
JIM KERSHNER

Preheat oven to 400°F. Using 1- to 2-inch cookie cutter, cut 4 rounds from each slice of bread. Combine next 4 ingredients in bowl. Using fork, mix just to blend. Divide mixture among 16 rounds, spreading evenly. Arrange on baking sheet and bake until golden brown, about 15 minutes. Serve immediately.

Serve with dry sparkling wine, such as Champagne, Cava, or Prosecco.

BLACK WALNUT BARS
WITH SUNFLOWER SEEDS

The black walnuts of Kansas are famous, and the sunflower is the Kansas state flower. Reta, a Kansas native, brings the two together deliciously in these rich bar cookies. If you can't find black walnuts, regular ones will do nicely.

Makes 30

Crust

Butter for pan

1½ cups all purpose flour

½ cup finely chopped black walnuts

⅓ cup (firmly packed) golden brown sugar

½ teaspoon salt

¾ cup (1½ sticks) chilled unsalted butter, cut into small pieces

Filling

4 large eggs

1 cup (firmly packed) golden brown sugar

1 cup dark corn syrup

¼ cup (½ stick) butter, melted

1 teaspoon vanilla extract

¼ teaspoon salt

1 cup coarsely chopped black walnuts

½ cup roasted unsalted shelled sunflower seeds

For crust: Preheat oven to 350°F. Lightly butter 13x9-inch baking pan. Combine flour, walnuts, sugar, and salt in large bowl. Using pastry blender or 2 knives, cut in butter until mixture is crumbly. Press mixture onto bottom of prepared pan. Bake until crust is golden brown, about 20 minutes.

Meanwhile, for filling: Whisk eggs, brown sugar, corn syrup, melted butter, vanilla, and salt in large bowl until smooth. Gently stir in walnuts and sunflower seeds. Pour mixture over hot crust. Bake until filling is set, about 35 minutes.

Cool in pan on rack. Cut into bars. (Can be prepared 3 days ahead; store in airtight container. Can be prepared 2 weeks ahead; wrap tightly and keep frozen.)

Serve with coffee, tea, milk, hot chocolate, or juice.

Submitted by:
RETA COFFMAN

BLUEGRASS HOT BROWN

The Brown Hotel in Louisville, Kentucky, is home to a locally famous sandwich known as the Hot Brown. The sandwich was created by hotel chef Fred K. Schmidt in the late 1920s as a change-of-pace snack for the social set who listened to the hotel band. The original recipe—for an open-face turkey sandwich covered in a Mornay sauce and garnished with bacon and pimiento—was an instant hit, and it has been around in one version or another (including this one created by John T. McCloud) ever since.

6 servings

Sauce
1 tablespoon butter
2 tablespoons all purpose flour
1 cup cold whole milk
1½ cups grated extra-sharp cheddar cheese
Salt and freshly ground black pepper

Sandwiches
6 slices sourdough bread, lightly toasted
12 thin slices deli ham (about 12 ounces)
12 thin slices deli turkey (about 12 ounces)
12 slices bacon, cooked until crisp
6 tomato slices

Submitted by:
JOHN T. McCLOUD

For sauce: Melt butter in heavy large saucepan over medium-low heat. Add flour and stir 1 minute. Add milk, increase heat, and bring to boil, whisking until smooth. Add cheese and whisk until melted and smooth. Season to taste with salt and pepper.

For sandwiches: Preheat broiler. Place each bread slice in individual gratin pan or on baking sheet.

Top each with 2 ham slices and 2 turkey slices. Cover each with ¼ cup sauce. Broil until hot and bubbly, about 2 minutes. Top each with 2 bacon slices and 1 tomato slice. Serve immediately.

Serve with bourbon.

CRAWFISH PIE

Crawfish is one of Louisiana's most important ingredients, and it shows up in a variety of culinary master-pieces, including this pie invented by Patricia Hale. This is wonderful for brunch, lunch, or supper, served with a salad. Cooked crawfish tails are readily available.

¼ cup (½ stick) butter
1 cup chopped onion
½ cup chopped green bell pepper
¼ cup chopped celery
2 green onions, chopped
2 tablespoons chopped fresh parsley
1 plum tomato, chopped
1½ teaspoons salt

½ teaspoon cayenne pepper
¼ cup all purpose flour
¼ cup white vermouth
1 8-ounce bottle clam juice
1½ pounds cooked crawfish tails
1 15-ounce package refrigerated pie crusts
(2 crusts)

6 to 8 servings

Preheat oven to 375°F. Melt butter in heavy large skillet over medium heat. Add next 5 ingredients and sauté until onions are translucent, about 8 minutes. Add tomato, salt, and cayenne and sauté until tomato is tender, about 5 minutes. Add flour and stir 1 minute. Add vermouth and bring to boil. Add clam juice and boil until thickened and slightly reduced, stirring occasionally, about 2 minutes. Add crawfish and stir to heat through. Line 9-inch-diameter pie dish with 1 pie crust; trim to ¼-inch overhang. Pour in crawfish mixture. Cover with other pie crust; trim to ½-inch overhang. Fold overhang under edge of bottom dough; crimp edges and make slits in top. Bake until crust is browned, about 45 minutes. Let stand 20 minutes before serving.

Serve with beer or white wine, such as Oregon Pinot Blanc.

Submitted by:
PATRICIA HALE

SPICED BLUEBERRY MUFFINS

Maine means blueberries, and blueberries mean muffins. These traditional breakfast and snack favorites have grown up with Martha and now come in handy as a treat for her young son. They're spiced with cinnamon, cardamom, coriander, and cloves and flavored with vanilla and almond extracts.

Makes 14

Oil for muffin cups
2 cups all purpose flour
½ cup sugar
1 tablespoon baking powder
½ teaspoon coarse sea salt
½ teaspoon ground cinnamon
½ teaspoon ground cardamom
½ teaspoon ground coriander
⅛ teaspoon ground cloves

1 large egg
⅓ cup grapeseed oil or vegetable oil
1 teaspoon vanilla extract
1 teaspoon almond extract
¾ cup whole milk
1 pint (2 cups) fresh blueberries or frozen blueberries, unthawed

1 tablespoon turbinado or raw sugar

Submitted by:
MARTHA BURR

Preheat oven to 425°F. Oil 14 standard muffin cups or line cups with paper liners. Sift flour, sugar, baking powder, salt, cinnamon, cardamom, coriander, and cloves into large bowl. Combine egg, oil, vanilla, and almond extract in another large bowl. Using fork or whisk, beat gently to blend. Beat in milk. Quickly stir flour mixture into egg mixture until just blended (do not overmix). Fold blueberries into batter.

Spoon batter into prepared muffin cups, filling each cup ⅔ full. Sprinkle batter lightly with sugar. Bake until toothpick inserted into center of muffin comes out clean, about 20 minutes. Serve warm or at room temperature. (Can be prepared 1 day ahead. Store in airtight container.)

Serve with coffee, tea, milk, hot chocolate, or juice.

OYSTER SPANAKOPITA

Chesapeake Bay oysters are just as delectable as Chesapeake crabs. Lisa grew up eating the bivalves from the bay in every way, shape, manner, and form. Here, she gives them a starring role in a luscious phyllo pie, also filled with ramps or green onions, spinach, and three cheeses.

12 to 16 servings

2 tablespoons (¼ stick) butter

2 pints (four 8-ounce packages) freshly shucked oysters

2 10-ounce packages frozen chopped spinach, thawed, drained, squeezed dry

1 cup chopped green onions or wild ramps

10 large eggs, beaten to blend

2 cups (firmly packed) crumbled feta cheese (about 12 ounces)

2 cups whole-milk ricotta cheese (about one 15-ounce container)

1 cup crumbled soft goat cheese (about 8 ounces)

2 tablespoons Dijon mustard

2 tablespoons (¼ stick) butter, melted

1 teaspoon freshly ground black pepper

½ teaspoon Tabasco sauce

¼ cup fresh lemon juice

10 tablespoons (1¼ sticks) butter, melted

12 sheets fresh phyllo pastry or frozen, thawed according to package instructions

Preheat oven to 350°F. Melt 2 tablespoons butter in heavy large skillet over medium-high heat. Add oysters with their liquid and cook 3 minutes. Drain oysters.

Combine next 10 ingredients in large bowl. Stir in lemon juice, then fold in sautéed oysters.

Brush bottom and sides of 15x10-inch baking dish with some of melted butter. Brush 1 phyllo sheet with some of melted butter. Top with another phyllo sheet. Brush with some of melted butter. Repeat until 6 phyllo sheets have been used. Line bottom and sides of prepared baking dish with layered phyllo. Top evenly with spinach-oyster mixture. Fold phyllo sides over filling and brush with some of melted butter. Cover with remaining phyllo sheets, brushing each with melted butter. (Can be assembled 6 hours ahead. Cover and refrigerate.) Bake until phyllo is golden brown, about 1 hour. Let stand 15 minutes before cutting into squares.

Serve with white wine, such as Sauvignon Blanc.

Submitted by:
LISA ESPADA

CAPE COD SCROD
WITH CRANBERRY RELISH & MINT

Massachusetts is known for its large haul of scrod and its large harvest of cranberries. Gail, who works in finance but whose heart belongs to cooking, married these two native ingredients in this inventive dish. If you can't find scrod, you can use halibut, tilapia, or orange roughy instead.

6 servings

Relish

2 cups fresh cranberries
¾ cup chopped white onion
3 tablespoons (firmly packed) golden brown sugar
2 tablespoons fresh lime juice
2 jalapeño chiles, seeded, coarsely chopped
2 garlic cloves, minced
2 tablespoons water
Salt and freshly ground black pepper

Fish

6 5- to 6-ounce scrod fillets or steaks, 1 inch at thickest part
3 tablespoons fresh lime juice
2 tablespoons grated peeled fresh ginger
2 tablespoons soy sauce
2 tablespoons olive oil
Salt and freshly ground black pepper
2 tablespoons thinly sliced fresh mint leaves

Submitted by:
GAIL GOOLGASIAN

For relish: Combine first 6 ingredients in heavy medium saucepan and cook over medium heat until cranberries are tender and falling apart, stirring frequently, about 5 minutes. Transfer mixture to processor. Using on/off turns, pulse until mixture is coarsely pureed, adding water 1 tablespoon at a time to thin. Season to taste with salt and pepper. Let cool. (Can be prepared 4 days ahead. Cover and refrigerate.)

For fish: Preheat oven to 425°F. Grease baking sheet. Arrange fish on prepared sheet (if using fillets, place skin side down). Combine next 4 ingredients in small bowl. Brush fish generously with lime-ginger mixture. Season with salt and pepper. Cook 8 minutes. Brush fish again. Cook until fish is opaque, about 4 minutes. Set 1 piece of fish on each plate. Sprinkle fish with mint leaves. Spoon relish alongside fish.

Serve with white wine, such as Chardonnay.

SOUR CREAM COFFEE CAKE
WITH CHOCOLATE, WALNUTS & CHERRIES

This recipe is based on the memory of a sour cream coffee cake that Rosemary ate every weekend when she lived in California. When she moved to Michigan, she had to add cherries to honor the state's famous fruit, and because chocolate goes so well with cherries, she had to add that as well.

Cake
Butter for pan
Flour for pan
1 cup (2 sticks) unsalted butter, room temperature
2 cups sugar
2 large eggs
2 teaspoons baking powder
2 teaspoons vanilla extract
2 cups sour cream (one 16-ounce container)
3 cups all purpose flour
1 teaspoon baking soda
½ teaspoon salt

Topping
1 cup mini semisweet chocolate chips
1 cup (about 4 ounces) walnuts, toasted, chopped
¾ cup (about 5 ounces) dried tart cherries, chopped
¼ cup (firmly packed) golden brown sugar
1 tablespoon ground cinnamon

10 to 12 servings

For cake: Butter angel food cake pan. Line bottom with parchment paper; butter and flour paper, tapping out excess flour. Using electric mixer, cream butter and sugar in bowl. Beat in eggs 1 at a time. Stir baking powder and vanilla into sour cream in another bowl. Beat into egg mixture. Whisk flour, soda, and salt in another bowl. Add to creamed mixture, beating at low speed or using wooden spoon just to blend.

For topping: Combine all ingredients in bowl.

To assemble: Preheat oven to 350°F. Spoon half of batter evenly around bottom of prepared pan.

Sprinkle half of topping over batter in pan. Add remaining batter, then remaining topping. Bake until tester inserted into center of cake comes out clean, about 1½ hours (cake will be moist when done). Cool cake in pan on rack. Run knife around edges of cake; remove sides of pan. Using 2 spatulas, lift cake from pan bottom onto flat serving plate. (Can be prepared 4 days ahead. Wrap in plastic.)

Submitted by:
**ROSEMARY
HOLLANDER**

Serve with coffee, tea, milk, hot chocolate, or juice.

WILD RICE, TURKEY & VEGETABLE
HOTDISH

A homey casserole known as a hotdish is a Minnesota staple. Here, Wendy makes one that's a combination of the state's top ingredients—wild rice from the north; turkey from Worthington, her husband's hometown; and pine nuts, from the state tree.

8 servings

6 tablespoons (¾ stick) butter, divided
2 cups chopped celery
½ cup minced onion
½ cup sliced carrot
1 pound ground turkey
¼ pound mushrooms, sliced

½ cup all purpose flour
3 cups chicken broth
½ teaspoon dried thyme, crumbled
2 cups cooked wild rice
Salt and freshly ground black pepper
¼ cup pine nuts

Submitted by:
WENDY L. NICKEL

Preheat oven to 350°F. Melt 2 tablespoons butter in heavy large skillet over medium-high heat. Add celery, onion, and carrot and sauté until tender, about 5 minutes. Transfer vegetables to large bowl. Melt 1 tablespoon butter in same skillet. Add turkey and brown well, breaking up with wooden spoon, about 5 minutes. Transfer to bowl with vegetables. Melt 1 tablespoon butter in same skillet. Add mushrooms and sauté until browned, about 5 minutes. Transfer to bowl with vegetables and turkey. Melt remaining 2 tablespoons butter in same skillet. Sprinkle flour over butter and cook 1 minute, stirring frequently. Add chicken broth and thyme to skillet and boil until thickened, about 3 minutes. Pour over vegetables and turkey in bowl. Stir in rice. Season with salt and pepper. Spoon into 3-quart casserole dish. Bake 30 minutes. Sprinkle with pine nuts. Bake 15 minutes longer. Serve immediately.

Serve with dry rosé.

MUDDY RIVER MOCHA BARS

Lorie, a frequent cooking contest competitor, named these triple-layer chocolate-pecan-marshmallow-coffee bars after the popular Mississippi Mud Cake, which is named after the muddy-looking Mississippi River.

Bottom Layer
Nonstick vegetable oil spray
- 1 cup semisweet chocolate chips
- ½ cup (1 stick) butter

- ¼ cup warm water
- 1 tablespoon instant coffee
- 3 large eggs
- 1 cup (firmly packed) golden brown sugar
- 1 teaspoon vanilla extract
- ½ teaspoon salt
- ⅔ cup all purpose flour

Middle Layer
- 2 7-ounce jars marshmallow creme
- 1½ cups finely crushed chocolate sandwich cookies or wafer cookies

Top Layer
- ¼ cup whole milk
- 1 tablespoon instant coffee
- ½ cup (1 stick) butter
- 3 tablespoons cocoa powder
- 1 teaspoon vanilla extract
- 3 cups powdered sugar
- 1 cup chopped pecans
Additional cocoa powder (for dusting)

Makes 36

For bottom layer: Preheat oven to 350°F. Spray 9x9-inch baking pan with nonstick spray. Combine chocolate chips and butter in heavy small saucepan over very low heat; stir until melted. Cool 10 minutes.

Pour ¼ cup warm water into large bowl. Add coffee and stir to dissolve. Add eggs, brown sugar, vanilla, and salt to coffee mixture and whisk until smooth. Blend in cooled chocolate mixture. Stir in flour, mixing well. Pour into prepared pan. Bake until puffed at edges and toothpick inserted into center comes out with moist crumbs attached, about 30 minutes.

For middle layer: Combine marshmallow creme and crushed cookies in bowl; stir to blend. Drop by even spoonfuls over warm bottom layer.

For top layer: Place milk in heavy medium saucepan over medium heat. Add coffee and stir to dissolve. Stir in butter and cocoa. Increase heat and bring to boil, stirring often. Remove from heat; mix in vanilla. Add powdered sugar and stir until smooth. Stir in pecans. Spoon warm mixture evenly over middle layer. Dust with cocoa powder. Refrigerate at least 2 hours before cutting into bars. (Can be prepared up to 3 days ahead. Store in airtight container.)

Submitted by:
LORIE ROACH

Serve with coffee, tea, milk, hot chocolate, or juice.

OZARK SPOON BREAD

Spoon bread is a classic side dish in the Show Me State. We added cheese to the original recipe for a savory twist. Domestic Asiago was our top choice, but white cheddar would be good, too. To make Carolyn's version, omit the cheese and serve with butter and maple syrup. Accompany with a salad for lunch, or with grilled meat, fish, or chicken for dinner.

8 servings

Butter for dish
2 cups whole milk, divided
1 cup yellow cornmeal
4 large eggs, separated
1½ cups grated Asiago cheese

2 tablespoons (¼ stick) butter
1 tablespoon minced fresh parsley
1 teaspoon baking powder
1 teaspoon salt

Submitted by:
CAROLYN HEWITT

Preheat oven to 375°F. Butter 8x8-inch glass baking dish or soufflé dish. Pour 1 cup milk into small bowl. Whisk in cornmeal. Pour remaining 1 cup milk into heavy medium saucepan; bring to simmer over low heat. Whisk in cornmeal mixture; stir over low heat until mixture thickens and boils, about 3 minutes. Stir in egg yolks, cheese, butter, parsley, baking powder, and salt. Place egg whites in clean bowl.

Using electric mixer, beat whites until stiff peaks form. Stir ¼ of whites into cornmeal mixture, then fold in remaining whites. Transfer mixture to prepared dish. Bake until puffed and brown, about 1 hour. Serve immediately.

Serve with white or red wine, depending on what the spoon bread is served with.

BUTTE PASTIES

Butte is a mining town that attracted immigrants from Cornwall, England, in the early 1900s. One of them was Edward's grandfather. The immigrants brought with them a culinary specialty called the Cornish pasty, which is a savory turnover usually filled with meat and vegetables. Edward often makes the pasty with elk supplied by his father, who likes to hunt.

Dough

 3 cups all purpose flour
 1 teaspoon salt
 1 cup (8 ounces) lard, cut into 1-inch
   pieces, frozen
 1 large egg beaten with ⅓ cup ice water

Filling

 1 pound skirt steak, cut crosswise into thin strips
 1 cup finely chopped onion
 ¾ cup finely chopped carrot
 ½ pound white rose potatoes, peeled, diced
 ¼ cup (½ stick) butter, melted
 1 tablespoon Dijon mustard
 1½ teaspoons salt
 1 teaspoon dried thyme, crumbled
 3 garlic cloves, minced

Assembly

 1 large egg yolk beaten with 1 tablespoon water

Makes 4 large pasties

For dough: Combine flour and salt in processor. Add lard and blend until mixture resembles coarse meal. Add egg-water mixture and blend until dough just comes together. Turn dough out onto lightly floured surface. Divide dough into 4 equal pieces; shape into 4 disks. Cover each disk with plastic wrap and refrigerate.

For filling: Combine all ingredients in large bowl; stir well.

To assemble: Preheat oven to 400°F. Roll out each dough disk between 2 sheets of parchment paper to 11-inch round. Remove parchment paper from top of each dough round. Divide filling among rounds, mounding in center on 1 side of each round. Brush dough edges with yolk mixture. Using bottom parchment sheet as aid, fold dough up over filling. Seal and crimp edges. Using parchment, slide pasties onto baking sheets. Bake 15 minutes. Reduce oven temperature to 325°F and continue baking until filling is tender when pierced with skewer and crust is golden brown, about 1 hour. Cool to room temperature before serving.

Serve with beer.

Submitted by:
EDWARD T. NICHOLLS

CORN- & MUSHROOM-STUFFED
SPICED PORK LOIN

Nebraska is a state where the family dinner is a tradition that will never go out of style. Steven carries on the tradition with this stylish dish that brings together two of Nebraska's stellar products, pork and corn.

6 to 8 servings

Spice Rub
1½ teaspoons freshly ground black pepper
½ teaspoon cayenne pepper
½ teaspoon coarse salt
½ teaspoon dry mustard
½ teaspoon paprika
½ teaspoon brown sugar

Pork
4 tablespoons olive oil, divided
1 medium Vidalia onion, diced
1 garlic clove, minced

1 portobello mushroom, stems and gills discarded, finely chopped (about ¾ cup)
2 cups fresh or frozen corn, divided
2 tablespoons chopped fresh parsley
2 tablespoons chopped fresh basil

2 ounces cream cheese, room temperature
Salt and freshly ground black pepper

1 3-pound pork loin, trimmed of fat and silver skin

¾ cup dry white wine
¾ cup chicken broth

Submitted by:
STEVEN GOBEL

For spice rub: Combine all ingredients in small bowl and set aside.

For pork: Heat 2 tablespoons olive oil in large skillet over medium-high heat. Add onion and garlic and sauté until onion is tender and slightly browned, about 5 minutes. Add mushroom and sauté until tender, about 3 minutes. Reduce heat to low. Stir in 1 cup corn, parsley, and basil and cook until corn is tender, about 8 minutes. Remove from heat and let cool.

Preheat oven to 425°F. Transfer corn mixture to processor. Add cream cheese and mix in, about 2 to 4 pulses. Transfer mixture to medium bowl. Stir in remaining 1 cup corn. Season to taste with salt and pepper.

Using sharp knife and starting at 1 long end, cut pork to within ¾ inch of opposite side. Open pork like book. Place between sheets of plastic wrap.

Using mallet, pound pork to 12x9-inch rectangle. Season with salt and pepper. Spread corn mixture evenly on pork loin, leaving ½-inch border. Starting at long end, roll pork tightly. Sprinkle all over with spice rub. Tie pork with kitchen string.

Heat remaining 2 tablespoons olive oil in heavy large skillet over medium heat. Add pork to pan and brown on all sides. Transfer pork to roasting pan. Roast until meat thermometer inserted into pork registers 150°F, about 50 minutes. Transfer pork to cutting board. Set roasting pan over medium-high heat. Add wine to pan and stir with wooden spoon, scraping up browned bits. Add broth and boil until liquid is reduced to 1 cup, about 5 minutes. Remove string from pork. Cut pork into slices. Place on platter. Pour pan juices over. Serve immediately.

Serve with red wine such as Pinot Noir.

STRIP STEAKS LAS VEGAS

Denizens of Nevada love their steaks, and this sophisticated yet simple recipe makes it easy to understand why. Gary uses balsamic vinegar, Worcestershire sauce, Madeira, ancho chile, and garlic in the luscious strip steak marinade.

¼ cup olive oil
¼ cup balsamic vinegar
¼ cup Worcestershire sauce
2 tablespoons Madeira
2 to 3 garlic cloves, pressed

1 teaspoon ground ancho chile, cayenne pepper, or paprika
2 12-ounce New York or Kansas City strip steaks

Salt and freshly ground black pepper

2 to 4 servings

Combine first 6 ingredients in glass baking dish. Add steaks and turn to coat with marinade. Refrigerate at least 3 hours or overnight, turning steaks occasionally.

Preheat broiler. Remove steaks from marinade. Season steaks with salt and pepper. Pour marinade remaining in dish into saucepan and bring to boil.

Broil steaks to desired doneness, about 5 minutes per side for medium-rare, basting with marinade from saucepan if desired. Serve immediately, either whole or cut into slices.

Serve with red wine, such as Cabernet Sauvignon.

Submitted by:
GARY R. CLIFTON

APPLE, WALNUT & MAPLE
CAKE-CRUMBLE

New Hampshire's iconic Old Man of the Mountain crumbled into a heap in May 2003, but his image remains on all the state road signs and license plates. This recipe is an homage to him, as well as a wonderful showcase for New Hampshire apples and maple syrup. Joan likes to make the crumble with terrific New Hampshire blueberries when they're in season.

6 to 8 servings

Cake
Butter for pan
Flour for pan
1 cup all purpose flour
1 teaspoon baking powder
1 teaspoon cinnamon
½ teaspoon salt
¼ cup (½ stick) unsalted butter,
    room temperature
⅔ cup sugar
1 large egg
⅓ cup milk
2 tablespoons pure maple syrup
3¾ pounds (about 4) tart green apples, peeled,
    thinly sliced (about 6 cups)
¾ cup walnuts

Topping
½ cup sugar
½ cup all purpose flour
¼ teaspoon salt
¼ teaspoon freshly grated nutmeg
¼ cup (½ stick) chilled unsalted butter, cut
    into small pieces
2 tablespoons pure maple syrup

Walnut or vanilla ice cream

Submitted by:
JOAN W. CHURCHILL

For cake: Preheat oven to 350°F. Butter and flour 8x8-inch glass baking dish. Sift flour, baking powder, cinnamon, and salt into medium bowl. Using electric mixer, beat butter and sugar in large bowl until light and creamy. Beat in egg. Beat in dry ingredients alternately with milk and syrup. Add apples to batter and stir well. Transfer to prepared dish. Sprinkle walnuts over batter.

For topping: Combine sugar, flour, salt, and nutmeg in bowl. Add butter. Using pastry blender or fingertips, cut butter in until mixture resembles coarse meal. Sprinkle topping over batter. Drizzle with maple syrup. Bake until tester inserted into center comes out clean, about 1 hour.

Serve cake-crumble warm with ice cream.

Serve with coffee, tea, milk, hot chocolate, or juice.

CREPE LASAGNA

From the home of one of America's most famous Italian-American populations, one of the best lasagnas ever. However, this is lasagna with a twist: It's made with crepes instead of pasta. Raffaella insists it's the lightest lasagna you'll ever taste.

8 to 10 servings

Sauce
- 3 tablespoons olive oil
- 1 onion, chopped
- 3 garlic cloves, minced
- 1 pound Italian turkey sausages, casings removed
- 3 14½-ounce cans diced tomatoes with Italian herbs
- ¼ cup finely chopped fresh parsley
- ¼ cup finely chopped fresh basil
- Salt and freshly ground black pepper

Crepes
- 1½ cups all purpose flour
- 1½ cups water
- 6 large eggs
- ½ teaspoon salt
- Nonstick vegetable oil spray

Assembly
- 2 pounds whole-milk ricotta cheese
- 1 cup grated Pecorino Romano cheese
- 2 large eggs
- 2 tablespoons finely chopped fresh parsley
- 2 tablespoons finely chopped fresh basil
- ½ teaspoon salt
- ¼ teaspoon freshly ground black pepper
- Pinch of freshly grated nutmeg
- 1 pound (two 8-ounce packages) shredded Italian cheese mixture

For sauce: Heat olive oil in heavy large pot over medium-high heat. Add onion and garlic and sauté until onion is tender, about 8 minutes. Add sausage and sauté until no longer pink, about 4 minutes. Add tomatoes with their juices, parsley, and basil. Season with salt and pepper. Simmer until slightly thickened, stirring occasionally, about 10 minutes.

For crepes: Combine flour, 1½ cups water, eggs, and salt in large bowl; whisk until well blended. Heat 10-inch-diameter nonstick crepe pan or skillet over medium-high heat until pan is very hot. Spray skillet with nonstick spray. Ladle batter (about ½ cup) into skillet, swirling skillet until batter coats bottom of pan; pour off excess batter. Cook until edges are dry. Turn crepe over and cook 30 seconds. Turn out onto plate. Repeat with remaining batter.

To assemble: Preheat oven to 350°F. Mix ricotta and next 7 ingredients in large bowl. Ladle ¼ of sauce onto bottom of 13x9-inch glass baking dish. Line bottom of pan with crepes (crepes will overlap). Top with half of ricotta mixture. Cover with ¼ of sauce. Sprinkle with ⅓ of shredded cheese. Layer with crepes. Top with remaining ricotta mixture. Cover with ¼ of sauce. Sprinkle with ⅓ of cheese. Layer with crepes (some crepes might not be needed). Cover with remaining sauce. Sprinkle with remaining cheese. Place dish on baking sheet. Bake 1 hour. Let stand 20 minutes before cutting into squares. (Can be prepared 3 days ahead. Cover and refrigerate. Reheat before serving.)

Serve with red wine, such as Zinfandel or California Sangiovese.

Submitted by:
RAFFAELLA VOLPE

MEXICAN CHOCOLATE, RAISIN & PECAN
BREAD PUDDING WITH STRAWBERRIES

As a little girl growing up in New Mexico, one of Cynthia's favorite treats was to nibble on small chunks of cinnamon-laced Mexican chocolate. Many years later, she decided to incorporate this unique ingredient, as well as her state's fabulous pecans, into an elegant dessert.

10 servings

Pudding
½ cup golden raisins
⅓ cup plus 4 teaspoons coffee-flavored liqueur (such as Kahlúa)
1 1-pound loaf bakery egg bread with raisins, heels removed, sliced, or 1 loaf storebought sliced raisin bread
¼ cup hot water
8 ounces Mexican chocolate (such as Ibarra), chopped
3 large eggs
¼ cup sugar
2 cups Mexican crema or whipped cream
2 teaspoons vanilla extract
½ teaspoon ground cinnamon
½ cup pecan pieces
Butter for dishes

Topping
2 1-pint containers strawberries, hulled, sliced
½ cup coffee-flavored liqueur (such as Kahlúa)
¼ cup chopped fresh mint

Garnish
1 cup Mexican crema or whipped cream
½ teaspoon vanilla extract

Submitted by:
CYNTHIA FOWLER

For pudding: Place raisins in small bowl. Pour ⅓ cup liqueur over. Let stand 1 hour or overnight.

Preheat oven to 350°F. Place bread slices on baking sheets and toast until golden brown, about 15 minutes. Crumble bread into bowl (yield should be about 4 cups).

Combine 4 teaspoons liqueur and ¼ cup hot water in top of double boiler set over simmering water. Add chocolate and simmer until melted, stirring frequently. Cool slightly.

Whisk eggs and sugar to blend in large bowl. Whisk in crema, vanilla, and cinnamon. Stir in melted chocolate mixture. Add crumbled bread and raisin mixture and mix well. Stir in pecans. Cover and refrigerate until bread absorbs custard, about 2 hours.

Butter ten ⅔-cup custard cups or soufflé dishes. Divide pudding mixture among cups. Place cups in large roasting pan. Add enough hot water to come halfway up sides of cups. Bake until puddings are set and puffed in center, about 40 minutes. Remove cups from water bath. Let come to room temperature. Cover and refrigerate until cold. (Can be prepared up to 3 days ahead.)

For topping: Combine strawberries, liqueur, and mint in large bowl.

For garnish: Mix crema with vanilla in small bowl. Bring puddings to room temperature. Run knife around edges of puddings. Unmold puddings onto dessert plates. Spoon strawberries over. Drizzle with vanilla crema.

Serve with coffee, tea, milk, hot chocolate, or juice.

ARTHUR'S HAMPTONS CHEESECAKE

The classic New York cheesecake with a graham cracker crust is delicious in any state. This recipe originated with Arthur's late wife, or perhaps her mother, but Arthur changed things a bit and made the cheesecake his own. Garnish with fresh seasonal berries for added color.

Crust

Butter for pan

1¼ cups graham cracker crumbs

¼ cup sugar

⅓ cup melted unsalted butter

Filling

3 8-ounce packages cream cheese, room temperature

1¼ cups sugar

Pinch of salt

4 large eggs, room temperature

¾ teaspoon almond extract

Topping

2 cups sour cream

½ cup sugar

1 teaspoon vanilla extract

Pinch of salt

10 to 12 servings

For crust: Position 1 rack in top third and 1 rack in bottom third of oven; preheat to 375°F. Butter 10-inch-diameter springform pan. Place cracker crumbs and sugar in bowl. Add melted butter and stir to blend well. Press mixture evenly over bottom of prepared pan. Bake until crust is golden at edges, about 6 minutes. Reduce oven temperature to 350°F.

For filling: Using electric mixer, beat cream cheese, sugar, and salt in bowl until smooth. Add eggs 1 at a time, beating well after each addition. Mix in almond extract. Transfer filling to crust.

Place a dish of water on top rack of oven. Place cheesecake on bottom rack. Bake until filling is gently set, about 45 minutes. Let cool 25 minutes.

For topping: Preheat oven to 350°F. Stir sour cream and sugar in medium bowl until smooth. Mix in vanilla and salt. Spread topping evenly over cheesecake. Bake 15 minutes. Let cool. Refrigerate until ready to serve. (Can be prepared up to 3 days ahead.)

Serve with coffee, tea, milk, hot chocolate, or juice.

Submitted by:
ARTHUR J. FRENCH

70

MOUNTAIN SHORT RIBS

Sally and eight of her girlfriends have cooked their way through a different cookbook every year for 14 years. What she didn't find in any of those books was this rib recipe, which she created for a family dinner. Ribs can be considered the state meat of North Carolina. Serve these with mashed potatoes or pasta.

8 to 10 servings

¼ cup dry red wine
¼ cup fresh lemon juice
¼ cup soy sauce
2 tablespoons Better Than Bouillon Beef Base
  or similar product

1 16-ounce package fresh baby carrots
1 10-ounce package frozen pearl onions
1 cup chopped celery
6 pounds meaty short ribs, cut into 2½-inch pieces
1 28-ounce can diced tomatoes

Submitted by:
SALLY YATES
RICHESON

Preheat oven to 300°F. Combine wine, lemon juice, and soy sauce in medium bowl. Stir in bouillon and set aside.

Place carrots, onions, and celery in heavy large roasting pan with lid. Top with short ribs. Pour tomatoes with their juices over. Add bouillon mixture.

Cover and bake until ribs are very tender, about 4 hours. (Can be prepared 3 days ahead. Cool, cover, and refrigerate. Defat if desired. Reheat in 350°F oven until heated through, about 45 minutes.)

Serve with red wine, such as Syrah or Petite Syrah.

NODAK HUNTER'S HASH

There's nothing like a hearty hash after hunting—or hiking or biking—in the wilds of North Dakota. Marshall, an avid hunter, created a recipe that's perfect for brunch, lunch, or supper. Each serving is topped with a fried or poached egg if desired.

Vegetable oil for baking sheet
1 pound spicy Italian sausages, casings removed
1 cup chopped onion
2 pounds russet potatoes, scrubbed, cut into
    ½-inch dice
1 small green bell pepper, diced

1 small red bell pepper, diced
4 garlic cloves, minced
½ teaspoon cayenne pepper
Salt
6 to 8 fried or poached eggs (optional)

6 to 8 servings

Preheat oven to 450°F. Oil large baking sheet. Cook sausage in heavy large nonstick skillet over medium heat until beginning to brown, breaking up with spoon, about 3 minutes. Add onion and cook until onion is tender and sausage is almost cooked through, about 5 minutes. Stir in potatoes, peppers, and garlic. Transfer mixture to prepared baking sheet. Roast until potatoes are tender, about 45 minutes. Stir in cayenne pepper. Season with salt. Serve immediately, topping with eggs if desired.

If serving for supper, serve with a red wine, such as Zinfandel.

Submitted by:
MARSHALL JOHNSON

SPICY APPLE-PORK BURGERS
WITH APPLE RELISH & SECRET SAUCE

Ohio is known for its pork, and Johnny Appleseed made his way through the state planting apple trees. No wonder Patt brought the two ingredients together in a modern twist on that old midwestern favorite: the burger. The versatile sour cream-mayonnaise sauce is flavored with mustard, cilantro, and chipotle hot sauce.

Makes 4

Burgers
1 pound ground pork
½ cup finely diced peeled apple
¼ cup finely diced onion
2 tablespoons chopped fresh parsley
1½ teaspoons ground cumin
1½ teaspoons paprika
1½ teaspoons chili powder
1 teaspoon salt
1 teaspoon grated lemon peel
2 tablespoons (¼ stick) butter

Sauce
¼ cup sour cream
¼ cup mayonnaise
2 tablespoons stone-ground mustard
1 tablespoon minced fresh cilantro
1 teaspoon chipotle hot sauce
Freshly ground black pepper

Relish
1½ cups finely diced peeled apple
2 tablespoons fresh lemon juice
1½ tablespoons olive oil
1½ teaspoons stone-ground mustard
1½ teaspoons sugar
½ teaspoon coarse salt
⅛ teaspoon paprika

Assembly
4 kaiser rolls, split, toasted
Cilantro leaves, fresh baby spinach leaves, or arugula leaves (optional)

Submitted by:
PATT KNOTTS

For burgers: Preheat oven to 350°F. Combine first 9 ingredients in large bowl. Shape into four 4-inch patties. Place butter in 13x9-inch baking dish. Melt butter in oven. Add patties to dish. Bake 15 minutes.

For sauce: Combine all ingredients in small bowl and stir well. (Can be prepared 3 days ahead. Cover and refrigerate.)

For relish: Combine all ingredients in medium bowl and stir well. (Can be prepared 8 hours ahead. Cover and refrigerate.)

To assemble: Spread both halves of each roll with sauce. Top four halves with burgers. Spoon relish over burgers. Cover with cilantro, spinach, or arugula if desired. Top with remaining roll halves. Serve.

Serve with beer or red wine, such as Zinfandel or Syrah.

CORNBREAD CASSEROLE

Cornbread casserole—chock-full of beef, beans, tomatoes, and seasonings—is a classic Midwestern dish and perfect family fare. If you like, do as Victoria does and add grated potatoes to the filling. We prefer it without, but either way, it's delicious.

6 to 8 servings

Filling

- 2 tablespoons olive oil
- 1 large onion, chopped
- 3 garlic cloves, chopped
- 1 pound lean ground beef
- 1 tablespoon chili powder
- 2 medium russet potatoes, peeled, grated (optional)
- 1 15-ounce can pinto beans, drained
- 1 14½-ounce can diced tomatoes with jalapeños
- 1 4-ounce can diced green chilies
- 1 tablespoon dried oregano, crumbled

Salt and freshly ground black pepper

Cornbread

- ½ cup all purpose flour
- ½ cup yellow cornmeal
- 1 teaspoon baking powder
- ½ teaspoon baking soda
- ½ teaspoon salt
- ½ teaspoon sugar
- 3 tablespoons olive oil
- 1 large egg
- ½ cup whole milk

Assembly

- 2 cups grated sharp cheddar cheese
- ⅓ cup sliced black olives (optional)

For filling: Preheat oven to 400°F. Heat oil in heavy 10-inch-diameter ovenproof skillet (preferably cast-iron) over medium heat. Add onion and sauté until translucent, about 8 minutes. Add garlic and sauté 1 minute. Add ground beef and chili powder and cook until meat is no longer pink, breaking up meat with spoon, about 4 minutes. Mix in potatoes (if desired), pinto beans, tomatoes with their juices, chilies, and oregano and simmer until slightly thickened, stirring occasionally, about 10 minutes. Season to taste with salt and pepper. (Can be prepared 2 days ahead. Cover and refrigerate. Reheat before continuing.)

For cornbread: Whisk first 6 ingredients to blend in small bowl. Pour oil into medium bowl. Add egg and whisk until foamy. Stir in milk. Stir in dry ingredients.

To assemble: Sprinkle cheese over meat mixture. Add olives if desired. Carefully spoon cornbread mixture evenly over top. Bake until cornbread begins to brown, about 15 minutes. Serve immediately.

Serve with beer.

Submitted by:
VICTORIA ARNOLD

BAKED PEARS
WITH CRANBERRY-RED WINE GLAZE

Did you know that pears are Oregon's state fruit? Here, Barbara combines them with cranberry juice (cranberries grow in southwest Oregon) and red wine (from the state's Willamette Valley) in this simple yet spectacular dessert. Oh yes, and everything is finished off with ice cream (from Tillamook, on the west coast).

6 servings

6 large firm but ripe Bosc pears (about 3½ pounds total)
¾ cup cranberry juice cocktail
¾ cup dry red wine (such as Oregon Pinot Noir)
½ cup sugar
1 cinnamon stick
2 teaspoons grated orange peel
Vanilla ice cream

Submitted by:
BARBARA
GROSSMANN

Preheat oven to 350°F. Core pears from bottom with melon baller. Slice bottoms off pears so fruit will stand up in dish. Peel pears, leaving stems on. Set pears in 8x8x2-inch baking dish. Combine cranberry juice and next 4 ingredients in heavy medium saucepan over medium heat and stir to blend. Pour mixture over pears. Bake pears until tender when pierced with fork, about 1 hour, basting pears every 15 minutes. Transfer pears to plates. Pour liquid in baking pan into saucepan and simmer until reduced to ½ cup, about 3 minutes. Pour sauce over pears. Serve immediately with vanilla ice cream.

Serve with red wine, such as Oregon Pinot Noir or pear eau-de-vie.

81

SPINACH, RAISIN, ANCHOVY & CHEESE
PIZZA

Pennsylvania's large, proud Italian-American population loves to cook and eat specialties such as this pizza. This recipe originated with Carol's Italian immigrant maternal grandmother, who made the pie every Christmas Eve. Even as a child, Carol loved the unusual sweet and savory flavor combination. For a change, try Swiss chard instead of spinach.

Olive oil for pan
1 pound fresh or thawed frozen pizza dough

2 tablespoons olive oil
6 garlic cloves, minced
1 9-ounce bag fresh spinach leaves
¼ cup golden raisins
¼ teaspoon dried crushed red pepper
2 tablespoons torn fresh basil leaves

1 teaspoon minced fresh rosemary
Salt and freshly ground black pepper
6 oil-packed anchovies soaked in 2 tablespoons milk, drained, rinsed, chopped
1 cup (firmly packed) grated part-skim mozzarella cheese
¼ cup freshly shaved Parmesan cheese

6 to 8 appetizer servings
or 4 main-course servings

Brush baking sheet with olive oil. Using fingers, press dough into pan, stretching from middle out to sides until dough is 11-inch round. Let stand until dough is slightly springy to touch, about 20 minutes.

Preheat oven to 425°F. Heat 2 tablespoons olive oil in heavy large skillet over medium heat. Add garlic and sauté until tender, about 2 minutes. Add spinach, raisins, and crushed red pepper and sauté until spinach is wilted, about 4 minutes. Spread spinach mixture over pizza dough. Sprinkle with basil and rosemary. Season with salt and pepper. Top with anchovies. Layer with cheeses. Bake until crust is brown, about 20 minutes. Serve immediately.

Submitted by:
CAROL A. FAZIO

Serve with soda pop, beer, or red wine, such as Zinfandel.

DRIED FRUIT, NUT & SPICE CAKE
WITH RUM

Jennifer wanted to impress her British boyfriend, for whom fruitcake is a traditional treat, but she couldn't bear the standard leaden loaf filled with candied fruit. So she decided to create a cake more suited to American tastes, one that was much lighter and infused with many different spices. The result is a creation that impresses Rhode Islanders as much as it does those on the other side of "the pond." There's nothing quite like this spicy, fruity, rummy cake with a cup of hot tea to warm up a cold New England day.

Makes 2 loaves

Fruit
1⅓ cups raisins (about 6 ounces)
1 cup (scant) coarsely chopped dried apple slices (about 3 ounces)
¾ cup dried tart cherries (about 3½ ounces)
⅔ cup dried cranberries (about 3 ounces)
⅔ cup diced dried pears (about 3 ounces)
⅔ cup diced dried apricots (about 3 ounces)
½ cup sugar
⅓ cup dark rum
1½ cups (about) boiling water

Cake
Butter for pans
Flour for pans
1 cup all purpose flour
1 teaspoon ground cinnamon
½ teaspoon freshly grated nutmeg
¼ teaspoon ground mace
¼ teaspoon ground allspice
¼ teaspoon ground cardamom
¼ teaspoon ground cloves
¼ teaspoon baking soda
1¼ cups sugar
½ cup (1 stick) unsalted butter
2 large eggs
1 tablespoon dark rum
¾ cup chopped pecans (about 3 ounces)
¾ cup chopped walnuts (about 3 ounces)
Powdered sugar

Submitted by:
JENNIFER LUXMOORE

For fruit: Combine all fruit in large bowl. Add sugar and stir to coat fruit well. Blend in rum. Add enough boiling water to almost cover fruit. Let stand at room temperature until fruit is plump, at least 2 hours or overnight.

For cake: Preheat oven to 300°F. Butter and flour two 8 x 4 1/2 x 2 3/4-inch loaf pans. Combine 1 cup flour, all spices, and baking soda in bowl. Using heavy-duty mixer or electric mixer, cream sugar and butter in another bowl. Add eggs and rum and blend well.

Add flour mixture and beat until smooth. Add undrained fruit and nuts to batter and mix well with wooden spoon. Pour batter into prepared pans. Bake until toothpick inserted into center comes out clean, about 1 3/4 hours. Cool in pans on rack. (Can be prepared up to 1 month ahead. Wrap in plastic and store in cool dry place.) Dust cake with powdered sugar before serving.

Serve with coffee, tea, milk, hot chocolate, or juice.

SHRIMP, GRITS & CHEDDAR
GRATIN

Shrimp and grits is the quintessential low-country dish, combining the state's two best-known ingredients. Shrimp is vital to South Carolina's coastal economy. The shrimping season is seven months long, with the peak season being from July through October. And St. George holds the World Grits Festival each spring.

8 servings

3 tablespoons chopped fresh thyme or
   1 tablespoon dried thyme, crumbled
3 tablespoons dry white wine
1 tablespoon olive oil
5 garlic cloves, minced
1 pound uncooked large shrimp,
   peeled, deveined

Butter for dish
4 cups water
1 teaspoon salt
1 cup quick-cooking grits
⅔ cup whole milk
1¼ cups shredded white cheddar cheese
¼ cup (½ stick) butter
1 teaspoon Worcestershire sauce
¼ teaspoon cayenne pepper
4 large eggs, beaten to blend
1 teaspoon paprika

Combine first 4 ingredients in bowl. Add shrimp and stir to coat. Cover and refrigerate 20 minutes.

Preheat oven to 350°F. Butter 13x9-inch glass baking dish. Bring 4 cups water and salt to boil in heavy large saucepan. Stir in grits and return to boil. Cover, reduce heat, and simmer 5 minutes, stirring occasionally. Remove from heat. Stir in milk. Add next 4 ingredients, stirring until cheese and butter melt. Add eggs and mix well. Fold shrimp with any accumulated liquid into grits mixture. Spoon mixture into prepared dish. Sprinkle with paprika. Bake until heated through and lightly browned, about 45 minutes. Let stand 5 minutes before serving.

Serve with white wine, such as Oregon Pinot Gris.

Submitted by:
CANDACE
McMENAMIN

HOME ON THE RANGE
BUFFALO DIP

This delectable dip is an homage to the buffalo that roam the range of this great state, and to the flavors of buffalo wings: chicken, hot sauce, and blue cheese. It is also unbelievably easy to prepare. Joan cautions that if you serve the dip as an appetizer, you might not need to serve dinner.

6 to 8 servings

2 cups shredded cooked chicken
4 ounces cold cream cheese, cut into small cubes
½ cup buffalo wing hot sauce or barbecue sauce
⅓ cup thick blue cheese salad dressing

1 cup shredded mozzarella cheese
Celery sticks
Crackers
French bread slices

Submitted by:
JOAN PIERONI

Preheat oven to 350°F. Oil 9-inch-diameter pie dish. Layer first 5 ingredients in prepared pie dish in order listed, ending with mozzarella. Bake until hot and bubbly, about 20 minutes. Serve with celery, crackers, and bread.

Serve with cocktails.

MELISSA'S SWEET ROSE CAKE

In the old South, cakes are integrated into everyday life. All special occasions—whether weddings, reunions, baby showers, teas, fish fries, revivals, or Sunday dinners—call for special cakes. This pretty and elegant layer cake made with rose petal jam and rose water (both can be found at international markets) is very much part of the Southern cake baking tradition. Melissa created it to honor her grandmother, who loved roses.

8 to 10 servings

Cake
Butter for pans
Flour for pans
2 cups all purpose flour
2 teaspoons baking powder
¼ teaspoon salt
6 large egg whites
¾ cup whole milk
1½ teaspoons vanilla extract
1½ teaspoons rose water
¾ cup (1½ sticks) butter, room temperature
1½ cups sugar

Frosting
3 cups heavy cream
½ cup sugar
2 teaspoons vanilla extract
2 teaspoons rose water

Filling
¾ cup rose petal jam (or raspberry jam, if desired)

For cake: Preheat oven to 350°F. Butter and flour two 9-inch-diameter cake pans. Combine 2 cups flour, baking powder, and salt in medium bowl. Whisk egg whites, milk, vanilla and rose water in another medium bowl. Using electric mixer, beat butter and sugar in large bowl until fluffy, about 5 minutes. Beat in flour mixture in 3 additions alternately with egg white mixture in 2 additions. Using spatula, scrape down bowl and beaters often. Divide batter between prepared pans. Bake until toothpick inserted into center of cake comes out clean, about 25 minutes. Cool cakes in pans 10 minutes, then remove cakes from pans and cool completely on racks.

For frosting: Using whisk or electric mixer, beat all ingredients in large bowl until thick.

For filling and to assemble: Slice each cake horizontally in half. Set 1 bottom cake half on cake plate. Spread with ¼ cup jam, then 1 cup frosting and top with cake half. Repeat layering process 2 more times, ending with cake. Cover top and sides with remaining frosting. (Can be prepared 1 day ahead. Cover and refrigerate.) Cut into thin slices to serve.

Serve with dry sparkling wine, such as Champagne, Cava, or Prosecco.

Submitted by:
MELISSA THORNTON

90

CHICKEN ENCHILADAS
WITH SOUR CREAM, CILANTRO & GREEN SAUCE

What speaks louder of the Hispanic heritage in the great state of Texas than enchiladas? Chicken and sour cream enchiladas are Derrelynn's favorite, and she also loves a chicken, tomatillo, and cilantro soup that she used to eat when she lived along the Texas-Mexico border. So she put the two together to come up with this winning recipe. Garnish with black olives if you like.

8 servings

Olive oil for dish
4   skinless boneless chicken breast halves
    (about 1¼ pounds), boiled, chopped
4   cups grated Monterey Jack cheese, divided
1   cup plus 2 tablespoons chopped fresh cilantro
1   7-ounce can diced green chilies
1   tablespoon ground cumin

Salt and freshly ground black pepper
2   tablespoons (or more) olive oil
12 6-inch corn tortillas

1   28-ounce can green chile enchilada sauce
1   7-ounce can salsa verde
¾   cup sour cream

Submitted by:
DERRELYNN
PERRYMAN SPERBERG

Preheat oven to 400°F. Oil 13x9-inch baking dish. Place cooked chicken, 2 cups cheese, 1 cup cilantro, green chilies, and cumin in bowl. Stir to blend. Season to taste with salt and pepper. Heat 2 tablespoons olive oil in heavy large skillet. Fry tortillas in batches (do not crowd) until pliable, a few seconds on each side, adding more oil to skillet as needed. Transfer tortillas to plate.

Bring enchilada sauce and salsa verde to simmer in same skillet. Spoon ¼ cup of sauce into prepared dish. Quickly dip tortillas into remaining sauce (do not overdip or tortillas will fall apart). Divide chicken mixture among dipped tortillas (scant ½ cup per tortilla). Roll tortillas up, enclosing filling. Place enchiladas, seam side down, in prepared dish. Stir sour cream into remaining sauce. Pour over enchiladas. Sprinkle with remaining 2 cups cheese. Bake until enchiladas are heated through, 25 to 30 minutes. (Can be prepared up to 2 days ahead. Cool, cover, and refrigerate. Reheat before serving.) Garnish with 2 remaining tablespoons cilantro and serve.

Serve with beer or Margaritas.

SUNDAY SUPPER ROAST CHICKEN
WITH VEGETABLES

Family dinners are very important in Utah, and chicken is a favorite for Sunday supper. Beverly Jo says that there's nothing better than coming in from a day in the Utah snow and smelling chicken roasting with fresh vegetables and herbs.

4 to 6 servings

1   6- to 7-pound roasting chicken, cleaned
Poultry seasoning
Salt and freshly ground black pepper

¼ cup (½ stick) butter, cut into 4 pieces
4   fresh sage leaves
2   tablespoons Worcestershire sauce
2   tablespoons chopped fresh sage
1   tablespoon chopped fresh parsley
1   tablespoon chopped fresh chives
1   tablespoon chopped fresh thyme
1   teaspoon freshly ground black pepper
¾ cup (1½ sticks) butter, melted

1¼ pounds golf-ball-size red potatoes, halved
1   pound large carrots, peeled, cut into 2-inch pieces
1   large onion, cut into 8 pieces

¾ pound brussels sprouts, trimmed, with X cut into each core

Preheat oven to 375°F. Place chicken in large roasting pan. Sprinkle chicken inside and out with poultry seasoning, salt, and pepper.

Using fingers, gently separate breast skin from meat. Place 2 butter pieces and 2 sage leaves between skin and meat on each breast. Stir Worcestershire sauce, all herbs, and pepper into melted butter. Baste chicken generously with some of melted butter mixture. Sprinkle with salt and pepper. Roast 45 minutes.

Combine potatoes, carrots, and onion in bowl. Toss with some of remaining melted butter mixture. Place vegetables in roasting pan with chicken. Baste chicken with some of remaining melted butter mixture. Roast until meat thermometer registers 180°F when inserted into thigh without touching bone, 45 minutes to 1 hour.

Toss brussels sprouts with some of remaining melted butter mixture. Baste chicken with remaining melted butter mixture. Roast 10 minutes. Turn oven off. Transfer chicken to platter. Tent with foil to keep warm. Return pan to oven and roast vegetables 10 minutes longer.

Using slotted spoon, arrange vegetables around chicken on platter. Pour pan juices into gravy boat. Season with salt and pepper. Serve with chicken.

Serve with white wine, such as Chardonnay, or red wine, such as Cabernet Sauvignon or Cabernet Franc.

Submitted by:
BEVERLY JO MARTIN

NEW ENGLAND SPIDER CAKE
WITH MAPLE SYRUP

A "spider" is what a cast-iron skillet was called in Vermont during days gone by. And cornbread made in cast iron is typical of New England. Johanna's take on cornbread in a skillet, which is delicious for breakfast or dessert, also shows off pure Vermont maple syrup. Her kids return to Vermont from Los Angeles and Manhattan just to get a taste of this cake.

8 servings

2 cups whole milk
1 tablespoon distilled white vinegar or apple cider vinegar

1 cup all purpose flour
¾ cup yellow cornmeal
¾ cup sugar
½ teaspoon baking soda
½ teaspoon salt
2 large eggs

2 tablespoons (¼ stick) butter
1 cup whipping cream or heavy cream

Pure Vermont maple syrup

Submitted by:
JOHANNA ROBOHM

Preheat oven to 350°F. Combine milk and vinegar in medium bowl. Set aside to sour, about 10 minutes.

Combine flour, cornmeal, sugar, baking soda, and salt in another medium bowl. Whisk eggs into soured milk. Pour egg mixture into dry ingredients; stir to blend.

Melt butter in 10-inch-diameter cast-iron skillet. Pour batter into skillet. Pour cream into center of batter.

Carefully slide skillet into oven and bake until golden brown, 40 to 45 minutes.

Cut warm cake into wedges. Serve with maple syrup.

Serve with coffee, tea, milk, hot chocolate, or juice.

VERY SHERRY VIRGINIA HAM

The Virginia country ham tradition started when Captain Mallory Todd of Smithfield began dry-curing ham and bacon in 1779. Virginia hams are world-class and beloved on holiday tables throughout the world. Legend has it that Queen Victoria so adored Smithfield hams that she ordered six to be sent to her palace weekly. If you can get a dry-cured Virginia ham for this recipe, you should soak it in cold water overnight to get rid of the excess salt. You might want to change the water, depending on how salty the ham is. Mary Lou usually serves her ham with dressing patties made from cornbread, white bread, ham fat, herbs, and spices.

1 12- to 14-pound fully cooked bone-in ham
3 cups sweet Sherry
2 tablespoons whole cloves
3 bay leaves

¾ cup fresh breadcrumbs made from white bread
½ cup (firmly packed) golden brown sugar
¼ cup Dijon mustard
¼ cup distilled white vinegar
Additional whole cloves
1 cup water

18 to 20 servings

Preheat oven to 200°F. Place ham in heavy large roasting pan. Combine Sherry, 2 tablespoons cloves, and bay leaves and pour over ham. Cover with foil and bake 3 hours, turning ham once.

Increase oven temperature to 400°F. Combine breadcrumbs, brown sugar, mustard, and vinegar in bowl; stir with wooden spoon until paste forms.

Spread paste over ham. Stud ham with additional cloves. Pour 1 cup water into pan to prevent burning. Bake ham uncovered until browned, about 30 minutes. Slice ham thinly and serve with defatted pan juices.

Serve with dry rosé or white wine, such as dry Riesling.

Submitted by:
MARY LOU
NESTER-BAUMGARDNER

SALMON WITH PONZU GLAZE

Washington salmon is delicious indeed, and it is featured fabulously in this simple, Asian-tinged recipe. Lyne uses ponzu (a citrus soy sauce) as well as ketchup, Worcestershire sauce, ginger, mustard, and garlic in her marinade. Try the fish with basmati rice, an Asian-style noodle salad, or cole slaw.

6 servings

6 tablespoons (¾ stick) butter
6 tablespoons ponzu (citrus soy sauce)
¼ cup ketchup
2 teaspoons grated peeled fresh ginger
2 teaspoons dry mustard

2 garlic cloves, minced
1 teaspoon Worcestershire sauce
6 8- to 10-ounce salmon steaks
Fresh parsley sprigs
Lemon wedges

Submitted by:
LYNE B. ERVING

Preheat oven to 350°F. Melt butter in heavy medium saucepan. Stir in next 6 ingredients and bring to simmer. Set salmon steaks in glass or ceramic baking dish. Pour sauce over. Bake until salmon is just opaque, about 15 minutes. Place 1 salmon steak on each plate. Garnish with parsley and lemon. Serve immediately.

Serve with white wine, such as Sauvignon Blanc.

ROAST VENISON À LA PRICE

Venison is used extensively in rural West Virginia. If you don't hunt and your local butcher doesn't carry venison, you can substitute beef. Tina, an experienced hunter, says that ginger ale is the surprise ingredient in this dish. Make sure to start it at least eight hours ahead.

8 servings

2 cups ginger ale
½ cup olive oil, divided
½ cup (firmly packed) dark brown sugar
2 tablespoons soy sauce
1 tablespoon coarse salt
1 teaspoon whole black peppercorns
1 teaspoon cayenne pepper
1 teaspoon curry powder

½ teaspoon ground nutmeg
½ teaspoon ground allspice
2 fresh rosemary sprigs
2 bay leaves
1 large onion, quartered
1 garlic clove, crushed
1 3- to 4-pound venison roast, tied

Combine ginger ale, 1/4 cup olive oil, and next 12 ingredients in bowl large enough to hold roast. Add roast and turn to coat with marinade. Cover and refrigerate at least 8 hours or overnight.

Preheat oven to 375°F. Transfer roast from bowl to roasting pan large enough to hold meat. Remove onion quarters from bowl and place around roast. Pour off and set aside 1 cup marinade; discard remaining marinade. Mix reserved marinade with remaining 1/4 cup olive oil. Baste roast with 1/4 of mixture. Roast until meat thermometer inserted into thickest part of meat registers 125° to 130°F, about 1 hour 20 minutes, basting occasionally with remaining marinade mixture. Let roast rest for 15 minutes before carving.

Serve with red wine, such as Syrah.

Submitted by:
TINA M. PRICE

BEER, RYE, CARAWAY &
CHEDDAR PUFFS

Beer and cheddar cheese are two of Wisconsin's biggest exports, and they come together felicitously in these little golden puffs. We prepared them with ale, but you can use any kind of beer. Susan likes to fill the puffs with a creamy corned beef filling that is a Wisconsin favorite.

Makes about 2 dozen

1 cup beer

½ cup (1 stick) butter
1 garlic clove, pressed
½ cup all purpose flour
½ cup rye flour
½ teaspoon salt
¼ teaspoon freshly ground black pepper

5 large eggs
1 cup grated sharp cheddar cheese
2 tablespoons caraway seeds
2 tablespoons minced fresh parsley

Butter for baking sheets
1 teaspoon water

Submitted by:
SUSAN MARTIN

Pour beer into bowl. Let stand at room temperature 15 to 20 minutes, stirring occasionally.

Pour beer into heavy medium saucepan. Add butter and garlic and bring to boil. Combine both flours, salt, and pepper in bowl. Stir flour mixture into butter mixture and continue stirring until ingredients leave sides of pan and smooth ball forms, about 1 minute. Transfer mixture to large bowl. Using electric mixer, add 4 eggs 1 at a time, beating well after each addition. Stir in cheese, caraway seeds, and parsley. Let stand 1 hour.

Preheat oven to 375°F. Butter 2 baking sheets. Drop batter by rounded tablespoons or pipe batter into

1 1/2-inch mounds on prepared baking sheets, spacing 2 inches apart. Beat remaining egg with 1 teaspoon water in small bowl. Brush top of puffs with egg wash. Bake until puffed and golden brown, about 25 minutes. Transfer to wire rack. Immediately cut horizontal slit in each puff to allow steam to escape. Serve warm or at room temperature. (Can be prepared 1 day ahead. Store in airtight container.)

Serve with beer.

OVEN-FRIED CHICKEN
WITH HONEY-LEMON SAUCE

Wyoming has a thriving poultry industry and is known for its large production of honey. Linda was inspired by both, and by a desire to create a recipe for oven-fried chicken that tasted like real fried chicken. Serve this hearty but healthy main course with baked or roasted potatoes.

½ cup (1 stick) butter, melted, divided
½ cup honey
¼ cup fresh lemon juice
1 cup all purpose flour
2 teaspoons paprika

1 teaspoon salt
½ teaspoon freshly ground black pepper
1 2- to 3-pound chicken, cut into
  8 pieces, skinned

4 servings

Preheat oven to 400°F. Combine half of melted butter, honey, and lemon juice in bowl for sauce. Whisk flour, paprika, salt, and pepper in large bowl. Dredge chicken in seasoned flour, shaking off excess. Pour remaining melted butter into 13x9x2-inch baking dish. Arrange chicken in dish, turning to coat with butter. Cover and bake 25 minutes. Turn chicken. Pour sauce over chicken. Bake uncovered until chicken is cooked through, 20 to 25 minutes longer, basting occasionally with sauce in pan. Serve immediately.

Serve with white wine, such as Chardonnay.

Submitted by:
LINDA J.
ROBERTSON

INDEX BY COURSE

RECIPE INDEX

CRANBERRIES

Baked Pears with Cranberry-Red Wine Glaze, 80
Cape Cod Scrod with Cranberry Relish and Mint, 48

Crawfish Pie, 42

Creamy Halibut Dip with Serrano Chile, 10

Crepe Lasagna, 66

CUSTARDS AND PUDDINGS

Mexican Chocolate, Raisin, and Pecan Bread Pudding
with Strawberries, 68
New England Spider Cake with Maple Syrup, 96

DESSERTS

Apple, Walnut, and Maple Cake-Crumble, 64
Arthur's Hamptons Cheesecake, 70
Baked Pears with Cranberry-Red Wine Glaze, 80
Black Walnut Bars with Sunflower Seeds, 38
Dried Fruit, Nut, and Spice Cake with Rum, 84
Melissa's Sweet Rose Cake, 90
Mexican Chocolate, Raisin, and Pecan Bread Pudding
with Strawberries, 68
Muddy River Mocha Bars, 54
New England Spider Cake with Maple Syrup, 96
Peach Cobbler, 26
Sour Cream Coffee Cake with Chocolate, Walnuts,
and Cherries, 50
Western Slope Pear and Ginger Cake, 18

DIPS

Creamy Halibut Dip with Serrano Chile, 10
Home on the Range Buffalo Dip, 88

Dried Fruit, Nut, and Spice Cake with Rum, 84

EGGS

Crepe Lasagna, 66
Mexican Chocolate, Raisin, and Pecan Bread Pudding
with Strawberries, 68
Oyster Spanakopita, 46
Ozark Spoon Bread, 56

FISH

Cape Cod Scrod with Cranberry Relish and Mint, 48
Creamy Halibut Dip with Serrano Chile, 10
Roasted Grouper and Yellow Peppers with Key Lime,
Herbs, and Spices, 24
Salmon with Ponzu Glaze, 100
Spinach, Raisin, Anchovy, and Cheese Pizza, 82

FRUIT

Apple, Walnut, and Maple Cake-Crumble, 64
Baked Pears with Cranberry-Red Wine Glaze, 80
Cape Cod Scrod with Cranberry Relish and Mint, 48
Dried Fruit, Nut, and Spice Cake with Rum, 84
Island Fire-and-Ice Pulled Pork with Mango Salsa, 28
Mexican Chocolate, Raisin, and Pecan Bread Pudding
with Strawberries, 68
Oven-Fried Chicken with Honey-Lemon Sauce, 106
Peach Cobbler, 26
Roasted Grouper and Yellow Peppers with Key Lime,
Herbs, and Spices, 24
Sour Cream Coffee Cake with Chocolate, Walnuts,
and Cherries, 50
Spiced Blueberry Muffins, 44
Spicy Apple-Pork Burgers with Apple Relish and
Secret Sauce, 76
Spinach, Raisin, Anchovy, and Cheese Pizza, 82
Western Slope Pear and Ginger Cake, 18

Golden Valley Oven Chicken, 16

Gulf Coast Shrimp with Sweet Tomato Relish, 8

RECIPE INDEX

RECIPE INDEX

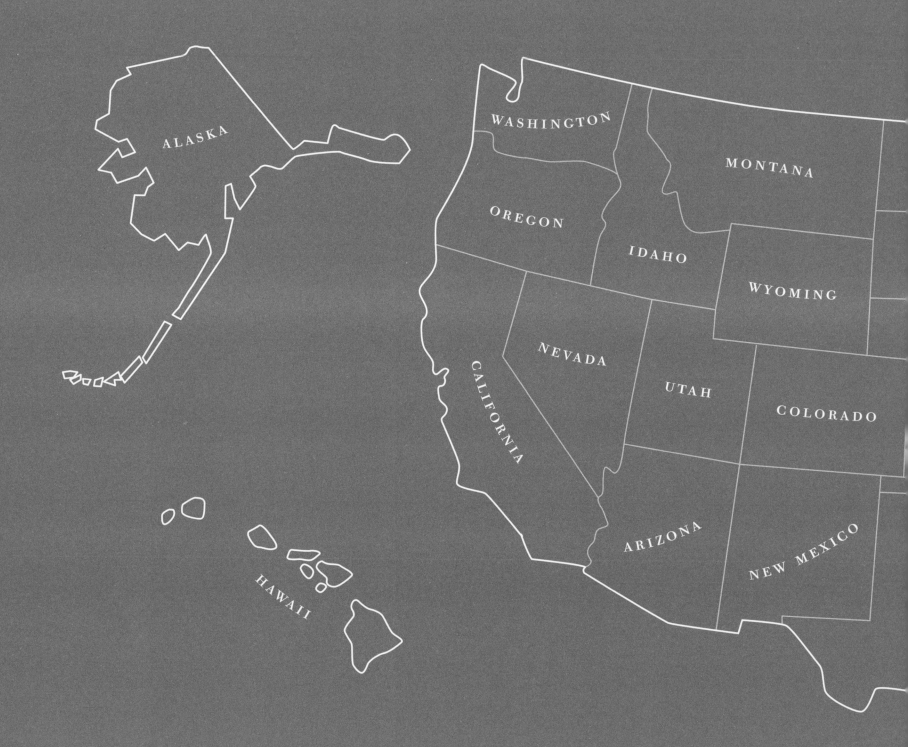